AUTISM ACROSS AGES

Insights for supporting Adults
and Children

By AVa Theodore, PhD

Copyright @ 2024 Ava Theodore, PhD

Legal Notice

Disclaimer Note

professional advice. The insights and suggestions in this book are based on general knowledge and personal stories, and while we strive for accuracy, we can't guarantee that they will apply to every individual situation.

Always consult with healthcare providers, educators, or other professionals when dealing with specific concerns or challenges. The personal success stories shared here reflect individual experiences and may not represent everyone's journey.

We hope you find this book valuable, but please use it as a guide rather than a definitive source. The authors and publisher are not responsible for any outcomes resulting from the use of this book. Thank you for understanding!

Table of Contents

Preface

This book, "Autism Across Ages: Insights for Supporting Adults and Children," aims to provide a comprehensive guide to understanding and supporting individuals with autism at different life stages.

The inspiration for this book stems from the countless stories of resilience, growth, and triumph shared by individuals with autism and their families. These stories highlight not only the challenges faced but also the remarkable achievements and unique perspectives that contribute to a more inclusive world.

Throughout this book, you will find practical strategies, expert insights, and heartfelt testimonials that illustrate the diverse experiences of those on the autism spectrum.

The testimonial stories shared in this book come from individuals and families I have had the privilege of working with during my years as a therapist. Each narrative reflects the unique challenges and triumphs experienced by those on the autism spectrum. These personal accounts illustrate the power of resilience, the impact of tailored therapeutic interventions, and the importance of unwavering support from loved ones. By sharing their journeys, these individuals offer invaluable insights and hope, demonstrating that with understanding and proper support, people with autism can thrive at every stage of life.

Chapter 1

Understanding Autism Spectrum Disorder (ASD)

Definition and Overview

Autism Spectrum Disorder (ASD) is a complex neurodevelopmental condition characterized by a range of symptoms that can affect social interaction, communication, and behavior. The term "spectrum" reflects the wide variability in challenges and strengths possessed by each person with autism. Some individuals with ASD may require substantial support in their daily lives, while others can live independently and exhibit exceptional talents.

The main signs of autism are restricted and repetitive patterns of behavior, interests, or hobbies, as well as difficulty with social communication and engagement. These symptoms normally start to show in early childhood, usually before the age of three, and they last the entirety of an individual's life. But there might be a lot of variation in how symptoms present and how severe they are

Autism is not a single condition but a spectrum of related disorders with a shared core of symptoms. This spectrum includes conditions previously recognized as distinct subtypes, such as Asperger's syndrome and Pervasive Developmental Disorder-Not Otherwise Specified (PDD-NOS). The American Psychiatric Association consolidated these subtypes into the broader category of ASD in the fifth edition of the Diagnostic and Statistical Manual of Mental Disorders (DSM-5) in 2013.

Historical Perspectives

The history of autism is a story of evolving understanding and changing perceptions. The term "autism" was first coined in 1911 by Swiss psychiatrist Eugen Bleuler to describe a symptom of severe schizophrenia, characterized by social withdrawal. However, autism was not acknowledged as a separate disorder until the 1940s.

In 1943, American psychiatrist Leo Kanner published a seminal paper describing 11

4

children with a unique set of behaviors, which he termed "early infantile autism." These children exhibited profound difficulties in social interaction, communication, and exhibited repetitive behaviors and restricted interests. Kanner's work laid the foundation for the recognition of autism as a distinct condition.

Around the same time, Austrian pediatrician Hans Asperger described a similar set of behaviors in older children with normal intelligence and language development, a condition later named Asperger's syndrome. Asperger's work was not widely known in the English-speaking world until the 1980s, leading to its inclusion in the DSM-IV in 1994 as a separate but related disorder.

Throughout the latter half of the 20th century, understanding and awareness of autism grew. The advocacy of parents, the establishment of autism-focused organizations, and the development of specialized educational programs contributed to greater recognition and support for individuals with autism. Advances in research and changes in diagnostic criteria have also played a crucial role in shaping our current understanding of the autism spectrum.

Prevalence and Statistics

Over the past few decades, there has been a notable increase in the prevalence of autism. According to the Centers for Disease Control and Prevention (CDC), approximately 1 in 54 children in the United States was identified with ASD in 2020. This represents a substantial increase from previous estimates, which reported rates of 1 in 150 children in 2000.

The reasons for this increase are multifaceted and include improved awareness and recognition of autism, changes in diagnostic criteria, and better diagnostic practices. Additionally, there is greater awareness of the full spectrum of autism, including individuals with milder forms of the condition who might have previously gone undiagnosed.

People of all racial, ethnic, and socioeconomic origins are affected by autism. However, research has shown disparities in diagnosis and access to services. Boys are about four times more likely to be diagnosed with autism than girls, though there is growing recognition that autism may present differently in females, leading to underdiagnosis or misdiagnosis.

Theories of Causes and Risk Factors

The exact cause of autism is not known, and it is likely that multiple factors contribute to its development. Research suggests that autism is a result of a combination of genetic and environmental influences.

Genetic Factors: Research has indicated that a substantial portion of autism development can be attributed to heredity. Twin and family studies indicate that if one child has autism, there is an increased risk that a sibling will also have the condition. Several genes have been associated with autism, and it is likely that multiple genes contribute to the risk. Some genetic syndromes and disorders, such as Fragile X syndrome and Rett syndrome, are also associated with autism.

Environmental variables: Although genetics is a major component, there may be other environmental variables that lead to the development of autism. Research has explored various prenatal and perinatal factors, such as advanced parental age, maternal infections during pregnancy, and complications during birth. Exposure to certain environmental toxins and medications during pregnancy has also been investigated as potential risk factors. However, it is important to note that vaccines have been extensively studied and have not been found to cause autism.

Neurological Differences: Brain imaging studies have revealed differences in the structure and function of the brains of individuals with autism. These differences are evident in areas of the brain involved in social interaction, communication, and behavior. For example, studies have found abnormalities in the connectivity and organization of neural networks in individuals with autism. These findings suggest that autism may involve atypical brain development and functioning.

Diagnosing Autism

Diagnosing autism involves a comprehensive evaluation by a team of healthcare professionals, including pediatricians, psychologists, neurologists, and speech-language pathologists. The diagnostic process typically includes:

Developmental Screening: This involves a brief assessment to identify children who may be at risk for developmental delays or disorders. Pediatricians often conduct developmental screenings during routine well-child visits.

Comprehensive Diagnostic Evaluation: If a child is identified as being at risk, a more detailed evaluation is conducted. This may include:

Clinical Observations: Direct observation of the child's behavior in various settings.
Parent and Caregiver Interviews: Gathering detailed information about the child's developmental history and current behavior.
Standardized Tests: Utilizing standardized diagnostic tools, such as the Autism Diagnostic Observation Schedule (ADOS) and the Autism Diagnostic Interview-Revised (ADI-R), to assess the child's behavior and symptoms.

Medical and neurological examinations: evaluating the child's general health and excluding the possibility of additional medical issues.

Improving outcomes for people with autism requires early identification and intervention. Early intervention programs can help children develop critical abilities and lessen the burden of symptoms. These programs may include behavioral therapies, occupational therapy, and speech and language therapy.

Part I: Autism in Children

Chapter 2

Early Signs and Diagnosis

Recognizing early signs of Autism Spectrum Disorder (ASD) is crucial for timely intervention and support. Autism can manifest in various ways, and its symptoms may vary widely among children. Understanding these signs and the diagnostic process is the first step toward ensuring that children with autism receive the help they need to thrive.

Recognizing Early Symptoms

Autism is typically diagnosed in early childhood, often between the ages of 2 and 4. However, some signs can be observed even earlier, sometimes as early as 12 months. Early recognition involves noticing deviations or delays in typical developmental milestones. These early signs often fall into three main categories: social communication, repetitive behaviors, and restricted interests.

1. Social Communication

Children with autism may show signs of social communication challenges early in life. These signs can include:

Lack of Eye Contact: One of the earliest indicators can be a noticeable lack of eye contact with caregivers and others.

Delayed Speech: Many children with autism experience delays in speech development. They might not babble as infants or may struggle to form words and sentences.

Nonverbal Communication: Children might not use gestures like pointing, waving, or nodding to communicate. They may also have difficulty understanding and using facial expressions.

Social Interaction: A child with autism may not show interest in playing with others, sharing experiences, or engaging in typical back-and-forth interactions. They might seem more interested in objects than people.

2. Repetitive Behaviors

Repetitive behaviors are a hallmark of autism and can appear in various forms:

Repetitive Movements: This can include hand-flapping, rocking, spinning, or other repetitive motor movements.

Fixated Interests: Children may exhibit a strong concentration on particular items, pursuits, or subjects, frequently to the detriment of other interests.

Ritualistic Behavior: They may insist on following the same routines or rituals and become very upset when these are disrupted.

3. Restricted Interests

Children with autism often have highly specific interests and may show a preference for certain toys, objects, or topics. These interests can be all-consuming and may dominate their play and conversations. They might prefer playing with parts of toys, like spinning the wheels of a car, rather than using the toy as intended.

Diagnostic Processes and Tools

Early diagnosis of autism involves a comprehensive evaluation by a team of specialists, including pediatricians, neurologists, psychologists, and speech-language pathologists. Usually, the diagnostic procedure consists of the following steps:

1. Developmental Screening:

During regular well-child visits, pediatricians conduct developmental screenings to check for signs of developmental delays. These screenings involve simple questionnaires or checklists that parents complete, which help identify children who might need further evaluation.

2. Comprehensive Diagnostic Evaluation:

If a screening indicates potential signs of autism, a more detailed evaluation is conducted. This evaluation involves:

Medical History: Gathering detailed information about the child's medical and developmental history, including family history of autism or other developmental disorders.
Observational Assessment: Observing the child's behavior and interactions in various settings to identify signs of autism.

Standardized Tests: Using standardized assessment tools, such as the Autism Diagnostic Observation Schedule (ADOS) and the Autism Diagnostic Interview-Revised (ADI-R), to evaluate the child's social, communication, and behavioral skills.

Hearing and Vision Tests: Conducting hearing and vision tests to rule out sensory impairments as a cause of developmental delays.

3. Multidisciplinary Team Assessment:

A team of specialists, including psychologists, speech-language pathologists, and occupational therapists, often conducts a multidisciplinary assessment. Each specialist evaluates different aspects of the child's development and behavior to provide a comprehensive understanding of the child's strengths and challenges.

4. Diagnosis and Feedback:

Based on the evaluation results, the team provides a diagnosis and discusses it with the parents or caregivers. They also provide recommendations for interventions, therapies, and support services tailored to the child's needs.

Importance of Early Diagnosis
It's important to diagnose autism early for a number of reasons:

1. Early Intervention

Interventions can start sooner the earlier autism is diagnosed.
Early intervention services, such as speech therapy, occupational therapy, and behavioral interventions, can significantly improve a child's development and quality of life.

2. Tailored Support:

A diagnosis provides a clear understanding of a child's needs, allowing parents and caregivers to seek appropriate support and services. This can include specialized educational programs, social skills training, and family support services.

3. Improved Outcomes:

Research has shown that children who receive early and intensive intervention tend to have better long-term outcomes. Early intervention can help improve communication skills, social interactions, and adaptive behaviors, leading to greater independence and success in adulthood.

Challenges in Early Diagnosis

Despite the benefits of early diagnosis, several challenges can hinder the process:

1. Variability in Symptoms:

Autism is a spectrum disorder, meaning symptoms can vary widely in severity and presentation. This variability can make it challenging to identify autism, especially in children with milder symptoms.

2. Limited Access to Services:

Access to diagnostic services and early intervention programs can be limited, particularly in rural or underserved areas. Long wait times for evaluations and a shortage of specialists can delay diagnosis and intervention.

3. Stigma and Misconceptions:

Stigma and misconceptions about autism can also be barriers to early diagnosis. Some parents may be hesitant to seek evaluation due to fear of labeling or misunderstanding autism's nature.

Supporting Families through Diagnosis

Receiving an autism diagnosis can be a significant and emotional experience for families. Providing support and resources to families during this time is essential:

1. Education and Information:

Providing accurate and comprehensive information about autism helps parents understand the diagnosis and what to expect. Educational materials, websites, and support groups can be valuable resources.

2. Emotional Support:

Connecting families with support groups, counseling services, and other parents of children with autism can provide emotional support and a sense of community. Sharing experiences and advice can help parents navigate the challenges of raising a child with autism.

3. Practical Guidance:

Offering practical guidance on accessing services, navigating the healthcare and education systems, and advocating for their child's needs is crucial. Case managers or advocates can assist families in coordinating care and accessing resources.

Supporting children with autism and their families requires an awareness of the early indicators of the disorder as well as a grasp of the diagnostic procedure. Early diagnosis enables more effective interventions, individualized support, and better results, enabling autistic children to realize their full potential. Despite the difficulties, empowering families and improving the lives of autistic children can be achieved by offering information, emotional support, and useful suggestions.

Chapter 3

Developmental Milestones and Challenges

Understanding the developmental milestones and challenges that children with Autism Spectrum Disorder (ASD) face is crucial for providing appropriate support and intervention. While children with ASD follow similar developmental trajectories as their neurotypical peers, the pace and nature of their development can differ significantly. This chapter explores the key developmental areas—social skills, communication, and sensory processing—and highlights the unique challenges and potential strategies for support.

Social and Communication Skills
Social Interaction

Social interaction is one of the core areas impacted by ASD. From an early age, children with autism may exhibit differences in how they engage with others. While some children might seem aloof or uninterested in social interactions, others may desire social connections but struggle to navigate social cues and conventions.

Developmental Milestones in Social Interaction:

Infancy (0-2 years): In the first two years of life, neurotypical children begin to show interest in others through eye contact, smiles, and cooing. They engage in simple interactive games like peek-a-boo. Children with ASD might show less interest in these activities, avoid eye contact, and not respond to their names.

Early Childhood (2-5 years): During these years, children typically start to play cooperatively with peers, take turns, and engage in imaginative play. Children with ASD might prefer solitary play, have difficulty understanding sharing and turn-taking, and struggle with pretend play.

School Age (6-12 years): As children grow, they form more complex friendships and understand social norms. They can work collaboratively in groups and participate in team sports. Children with ASD may continue to have challenges understanding social rules, making friends, and

interpreting body language and facial expressions.
Communication Skills

Communication, both verbal and non-verbal, is another area where children with ASD often face significant challenges. These challenges can range from delayed speech development to difficulties in understanding and using language appropriately.

Developmental Milestones in Communication:

Infancy (0-2 years): Typically developing infants begin to babble, gesture, and eventually say their first words by the end of the first year. Children with ASD might have delayed babbling, use fewer gestures, and may not speak until later.

Early Childhood (2-5 years): In this stage, children's vocabulary rapidly expands, and they start forming simple sentences. They also begin to understand and use non-verbal communication, such as pointing or nodding. Children with ASD might have limited vocabulary, speak in a monotone voice, or use repetitive language (echolalia).

School Age (6-12 years): By school age, children typically engage in complex conversations, understand humor, and adjust their language based on the social context. Children with ASD may have difficulties with pragmatic language, such as understanding sarcasm, making appropriate conversation, and interpreting social cues in discussions.

Sensory Processing and Behavioral Patterns

Sensory Processing

The way the brain understands and reacts to sensory data from the surroundings is known as sensory processing. Many children with ASD experience sensory processing differences, which can significantly impact their daily lives. These differences can manifest as either hypersensitivity (over-responsiveness) or hyposensitivity (under-responsiveness) to sensory stimuli.

Common Sensory Processing Challenges:

Hypersensitivity: Children who are hypersensitive might find certain sounds unbearably loud, lights too bright, or textures uncomfortable. This can lead to behaviors such

as covering their ears, avoiding certain foods, or becoming distressed in crowded environments. Hyposensitivity: On the other hand, children who are hyposensitive may not respond to sensory stimuli as expected. They might have a high pain tolerance, seek out intense sensory experiences (like spinning or crashing into things), or have difficulty with balance and coordination.
Behavioral Patterns

Behavioral patterns in children with ASD are often closely tied to their sensory experiences and communication challenges. Understanding these patterns can help caregivers and educators provide better support.

Common Behavioral Patterns:

Repetitive Behaviors: Many children with ASD engage in repetitive behaviors, such as hand-flapping, rocking, or repeating certain phrases. These behaviors, known as stimming, can help them manage sensory overload or provide comfort.
Routine and Predictability: Children with ASD often thrive on routine and predictability.

Sudden changes in their environment or schedule can be distressing and lead to meltdowns or withdrawal.

Challenging Behaviors: When children with ASD are unable to communicate their needs or are overwhelmed by sensory input, they might exhibit challenging behaviors such as tantrums, aggression, or self-injury. It is crucial to understand these behaviors as a form of communication and work on identifying their underlying causes.

Strategies for Support

Social Skills Interventions

Developing social skills is vital for children with ASD to build meaningful relationships and navigate social environments. Structured social skills training, social stories, and peer-mediated interventions can be effective.

Social Skills Training: Structured programs that teach specific social behaviors, such as greeting others, taking turns, and understanding social cues, can be beneficial. Role-playing and video modeling are often used in these programs.

Social tales: Social tales are brief narratives that explain proper reactions in various social contexts. They can help children with ASD understand social expectations and prepare for various scenarios.

Peer-Mediated Interventions: These interventions involve training typically developing peers to interact with and support their classmates with ASD. This can promote inclusion and help children with ASD develop social connections.

Communication Support

Enhancing communication skills in children with ASD requires a multifaceted approach, including speech therapy, augmentative and alternative communication (AAC), and parent training.

Speech Therapy: Speech-language pathologists can work with children on improving their speech and language skills. This might include exercises to enhance articulation, vocabulary, and sentence structure.

AAC: For non-verbal children or those with limited speech, AAC tools such as picture exchange communication systems (PECS), speech-generating devices, or communication apps can be invaluable.

Parent Training: Educating parents on communication strategies, such as using simple language, visual supports, and giving their child time to respond, can significantly enhance their child's communication abilities.

Sensory Integration Strategies

Addressing sensory processing challenges involves creating a supportive environment and teaching children self-regulation techniques.

Creating a Sensory-Friendly Environment: This might include using noise-canceling headphones, providing fidget toys, or having a quiet space where the child can retreat when overwhelmed.

Sensory Integration Therapy: Occupational therapists can assist youngsters in improving their ability to process sensory information by using sensory integration therapy. This could entail giving them controlled sensory input or engaging in activities that desensitize them to particular stimuli.

Self-Regulation Strategies: By teaching kids how to control their sensory needs through activities like deep pressure, breathing exercises, or sensory diets, you can help them learn how to handle sensory overload.

Providing effective support for children with ASD requires first having a thorough understanding of the developmental milestones and difficulties that these children encounter. Caregivers, educators, and therapists can adapt their approaches to meet the specific requirements of each child by acknowledging the distinct manner in which these children develop their social, communicative, and sensory processing skills. Children with ASD can advance significantly if they receive the appropriate assistance.

Chapter 4

Educational Strategies and Support

Inclusive Education

Inclusive education is a vital aspect of supporting children with Autism Spectrum Disorder (ASD). It is rooted in the belief that all students, regardless of their abilities, should learn together in the same age-appropriate classroom with the necessary support. Inclusion goes beyond mere physical presence in a classroom; it emphasizes active participation, access to the curriculum, and social integration.

One of the primary benefits of inclusive education is the promotion of social skills. Children with autism often struggle with social interactions, and being in a regular classroom allows them to observe and engage with their neurotypical peers. This interaction can significantly improve their social understanding and behaviors. Furthermore, inclusive settings foster empathy and acceptance among all students, helping to reduce stigma and build a more inclusive community.

However, inclusive education presents challenges. Teachers must adapt their teaching methods to accommodate diverse learning needs. This requires ongoing professional development and support. For instance, Universal Design for Learning (UDL) is an educational framework that guides the design of learning environments to accommodate individual learning differences. By using multiple means of representation, engagement, and expression, teachers can create lessons that are accessible to all students.

Individualized Education Plans (IEPs)

An Individualized Education Plan (IEP) is a legal document that outlines the educational goals, objectives, and services for a child with a disability. For children with autism, IEPs are essential in providing tailored educational support that meets their unique needs. The process of developing an IEP involves collaboration among parents, teachers, special education professionals, and, when appropriate, the student.

The IEP process begins with a comprehensive evaluation to determine the child's strengths, weaknesses, and needs. Based on this assessment, the IEP team sets specific, measurable goals. These goals may cover various areas, such as academic achievement, social skills, communication, and behavioral management. The IEP also specifies the services and accommodations the child will receive, such as speech therapy, occupational therapy, or the use of assistive technology.

Regular progress monitoring is crucial to ensure the child is meeting their IEP goals. The IEP team meets at least annually to review the child's progress and make necessary adjustments. This dynamic and responsive approach helps address the evolving needs of children with autism as they grow and develop.

Classroom Accommodations

Classroom accommodations are modifications and supports that help students with autism access the general education curriculum and participate fully in classroom activities. These accommodations can be categorized into environmental, instructional, and social supports.

Environmental Accommodations: These involve changes to the physical classroom setting to reduce sensory overload and create a more conducive learning environment. Examples include:

- Sensory-Friendly Spaces: Creating quiet corners or sensory rooms where students can take breaks and regulate their sensory input.
- Visual Supports: Using visual schedules, charts, and cues to help students understand routines and expectations.
- Seating Arrangements: Placing the student in a location that minimizes distractions, such as away from windows or high-traffic areas.

Instructional Accommodations: These adaptations modify how information is presented and how students demonstrate their knowledge. Examples include:

- Differentiated Instruction: Providing multiple ways to access content, such as through visual, auditory, and hands-on activities.
- Simplified Language: Using clear and concise language and breaking down instructions into smaller, manageable steps.
- Extended Time: Allowing additional time for completing assignments and tests.

Social Supports: These accommodations focus on enhancing social interactions and communication skills. Examples include:

- Peer Buddies: Pairing the student with a peer mentor to facilitate social interactions and provide support.
- Social Skills Training: Implementing programs that teach specific social skills, such as taking turns, making eye contact, and understanding social cues.
- Role-Playing Activities: Engaging students in role-playing scenarios to practice social interactions in a safe and structured environment.

Family Dynamics and Support Systems

Families play a crucial role in the education and development of children with autism. Understanding and addressing the dynamics within the family unit can significantly impact the child's success in school and beyond.

Sibling Relationships: Siblings of children with autism may experience a range of emotions, including pride, frustration, and jealousy. It's important for parents to recognize these feelings and provide support. Sibling support groups and counseling can offer a safe space for siblings to share their experiences and learn coping strategies.

Parental Roles and Coping Mechanisms: Parents of children with autism often take on multiple roles, including advocate, caregiver, and teacher. This can be overwhelming and stressful. Building a strong support network is essential. Support groups, counseling, and respite care can help parents manage stress and avoid burnout. Additionally, learning about autism and effective intervention strategies empowers parents to advocate effectively for their child's needs.

Community Resources: Connecting with community resources can provide additional

support for families. Organizations such as
Autism Speaks, the Autism Society, and local
support groups offer a wealth of information,
resources, and networking opportunities.
Schools can also partner with community
organizations to provide workshops, training,
and resources for families.

Testimonial Success Stories Children

Including testimonials from families and educators who have successfully navigated the educational journey with children with autism can provide hope and inspiration. These stories highlight practical strategies and the positive impact of early intervention and support.

Case Study

Emma's Journey to Inclusion Emma, a 6-year-old girl with autism, struggled with social interactions and sensory sensitivities. Her parents worked closely with her school to develop an IEP that included sensory breaks, a visual schedule, and speech therapy. Over time, Emma's social skills improved, and she began participating more in classroom activities. Her teachers noted significant progress in her communication skills, and Emma's self-confidence grew. Her story exemplifies the power of collaboration between families and schools in supporting children with autism.

Case Study

 Liam's Academic Success Liam, an 8-year-old boy with high-functioning autism, excelled academically but faced challenges with social skills. His IEP included a peer buddy program and social skills training. Liam's teachers used differentiated instruction to keep him engaged and challenged. With these supports, Liam not only thrived academically but also made meaningful friendships. His success story underscores the importance of addressing both academic and social needs.

These success stories demonstrate that with the right support and strategies, children with autism can achieve their full potential. The key is to recognize their unique strengths and provide the necessary accommodations to help them succeed.

A comprehensive strategy that incorporates inclusive education, customized lesson plans, and special classroom accommodations is needed to educate children with autism. A helpful and productive learning environment can only be established via cooperation between parents, educators, and other professionals. Children diagnosed with autism have specific needs that must be recognized and met in order to support their intellectual, social, and emotional development.

Chapter 5

Family Dynamics and Support Systems

The diagnosis of Autism Spectrum Disorder (ASD) in a child transforms the landscape of family life. Every member, from parents to siblings, must navigate a new reality filled with unique challenges and opportunities for growth. Understanding the dynamics at play and accessing the right support systems is crucial for fostering a nurturing environment where every family member can thrive.

Sibling Relationships
Sibling relationships are among the most enduring in life and can be profoundly affected by the presence of a child with autism. Siblings often find themselves grappling with mixed emotions, ranging from love and protectiveness to jealousy and resentment. It's essential to acknowledge and address these feelings to

maintain harmony and understanding within the family.

Positive Aspects:
Many siblings of children with autism develop a heightened sense of empathy and patience. They often become strong advocates for their sibling, demonstrating maturity beyond their years. These siblings learn to appreciate diversity and develop problem-solving skills as they find ways to interact and play with their autistic sibling.

Challenges:
On the other hand, siblings may also feel neglected due to the considerable attention their parents must give to the child with autism. They might struggle with feelings of embarrassment or frustration, especially in social settings where their sibling's behavior might be misunderstood. Ensuring that siblings receive adequate attention and support is crucial for their well-being.

Strategies for Support:

Open Communication: Encourage siblings to express their feelings and concerns. Create a safe space for them to talk about their experiences and emotions.Establish a secure environment so they can discuss their feelings and experiences.

Quality Time: Dedicate one-on-one time with each sibling to ensure they feel valued and important.
Education: Help siblings understand autism by providing age-appropriate information about the condition. This knowledge can foster empathy and reduce misconceptions.

Support Groups: Consider enrolling siblings in support groups where they can meet others in similar situations, share experiences, and gain support.

Parental Roles and Coping Mechanisms
Parents are often the primary caregivers and advocates for their child with autism. The journey from diagnosis to daily management can be overwhelming, and the emotional toll can be significant. Understanding and developing effective coping mechanisms is vital for maintaining parental mental health and overall family stability.

Emotional Impact:

Parents may experience a range of emotions, including grief, denial, anger, and acceptance. It's important to acknowledge these feelings as a normal part of the journey. Seeking support from other parents, therapists, or counselors can provide valuable outlets for processing these emotions.

Coping Strategies:

Self-Care: Prioritizing self-care is crucial. Parents should take time for activities they enjoy, maintain social connections, and ensure they get adequate rest and nutrition.
Support Networks: Building a robust support network, including family, friends, and professional support, can alleviate some of the burdens. Don't hesitate to seek assistance or help when needed.

Education and Advocacy: Becoming well-informed about autism and available resources empowers parents to advocate effectively for their child. Knowledge reduces anxiety and increases confidence in managing the condition.

Mindfulness and Stress Management: Practices such as mindfulness, meditation, and yoga can help manage stress and improve emotional resilience.

Community Resources
Accessing community resources can significantly enhance the support available to families of children with autism. These resources range from educational programs and support groups to specialized therapies and respite care.

Educational Programs:
Schools and community centers often offer programs specifically designed for children with autism. These programs provide tailored educational experiences that accommodate the unique learning styles and needs of autistic children.

Support Groups:
Support groups for parents, siblings, and even extended family members can provide a sense of community and shared experience. These groups offer emotional support, practical advice, and a platform for exchanging information about resources and strategies.

Therapies:
Various therapies, including speech therapy, occupational therapy, and behavioral therapy, play a crucial role in the development of children with autism. Community-based therapy programs can provide access to these essential services, often with the benefit of specialized knowledge and equipment.

Respite Care:
Caring for a child with autism can be demanding, and respite care offers parents a much-needed break. Respite care services provide temporary relief by offering professional caregiving, allowing parents to rest and recharge.

Building a Supportive Home Environment
Creating a supportive home environment is essential for the well-being of both the child with autism and the entire family. This involves establishing routines, modifying the physical space, and fostering positive interactions.

Structured Routines:
Children with autism often thrive on predictability. Establishing consistent routines for

daily activities, such as meals, bedtime, and therapy sessions, can provide a sense of security and reduce anxiety.

Physical Space Modifications:
Modifying the home environment to accommodate sensory sensitivities can greatly enhance comfort for a child with autism. This might include creating quiet spaces, using soft lighting, and reducing clutter and noise.

Positive Interactions:
Encouraging positive interactions through structured activities and play can strengthen family bonds. Setting aside time for family activities that everyone enjoys can promote inclusion and mutual understanding.

Visual Supports:
Using visual supports, such as schedules, charts, and social stories, can help children with autism understand and follow routines and expectations. These tools provide clear, visual cues that complement verbal instructions.

Navigating family dynamics and support systems is a continuous journey for families of children with autism. By fostering open communication, accessing community resources, and creating a supportive home environment, families can build a strong foundation that enables every member to thrive. Through understanding, empathy, and resilience, families can turn the challenges of autism into opportunities for growth and connection.

Chapter 6

Testimonial Success Stories: Children

Children diagnosed with Autism Spectrum Disorder (ASD) face a unique set of challenges that can often seem insurmountable. However, with the right support, understanding, and intervention, many children with autism achieve remarkable milestones and live fulfilling lives. This chapter is dedicated to sharing inspirational stories of children who have thrived despite their diagnosis, showcasing the power of resilience, personalized strategies, and unwavering support from families and communities.

A Journey of Communication

Liam was diagnosed with autism at the age of three. His parents, Sarah and Mark, were initially overwhelmed by the diagnosis and unsure of the future. Liam struggled with verbal communication, which made it difficult for him to express his needs and connect with others. Determined to help their son, Sarah and Mark immersed themselves in learning about autism and sought out early intervention programs.

Liam started speech therapy, and his parents learned about augmentative and alternative communication (AAC) devices. They introduced him to a tablet with a speech-generating app that allowed him to select words and phrases to communicate. Initially, progress was slow, but Liam's therapists and family celebrated every small achievement.

Over time, Liam began to use the AAC device more effectively. He could express his needs, share his feelings, and even participate in family conversations. His newfound ability to communicate reduced his frustration and opened up new opportunities for learning and social interaction. By the time Liam entered kindergarten, he was using his AAC device confidently and making friends. His story is a testament to the importance of early intervention and the transformative power of technology in enhancing communication for children with autism.

Overcoming Sensory Challenges

Emma was diagnosed with autism at the age of four. Her parents, Maria and Carlos, noticed early on that she had intense reactions to certain sensory stimuli. Loud noises, bright lights, and even the texture of her clothes could trigger meltdowns. These sensory challenges made it difficult for Emma to engage in everyday activities and enjoy typical childhood experiences.

Maria and Carlos worked closely with occupational therapists who specialized in sensory integration. They developed a personalized sensory diet for Emma, incorporating activities that helped her regulate her sensory input. The family created a sensory-friendly environment at home, with a quiet space where Emma could retreat when overwhelmed, and they used weighted blankets and noise-canceling headphones to help her feel more secure.

Emma's progress was gradual but steady. She began to tolerate more sensory input and developed coping strategies to manage her reactions. With support, she was able to participate in activities she once found unbearable, like attending birthday parties and going to the playground. Emma's story highlights the importance of understanding and addressing sensory needs, and the significant impact that tailored interventions can have on a child's ability to navigate their environment.

Academic Achievement Against the Odds

Jason was diagnosed with autism at the age of five. His parents, Lisa and David, were concerned about his future, particularly his ability to succeed in school. Jason had difficulty with attention, social interactions, and adapting to the structured environment of a classroom. His parents advocated for an Individualized Education Plan (IEP) that outlined specific accommodations and supports to help him thrive.

With the help of dedicated teachers and specialists, Jason received personalized instruction and therapies that catered to his unique learning style. He had a resource teacher who worked with him one-on-one and small group sessions that focused on social skills. The school also implemented visual schedules and breaks to help Jason manage his time and reduce anxiety.

Jason's progress was remarkable. By the end of first grade, he was reading above grade level and excelling in math. His teachers noted his enthusiasm for learning and his ability to tackle complex problems. While social interactions remained challenging, Jason's academic achievements boosted his confidence and provided a foundation for future success. His story illustrates the critical role of tailored educational strategies and the potential for children with autism to excel academically when given the right support.

Building Friendships and Social Skills

Lucy was diagnosed with autism at the age of six. Her parents, Jenna and Tom, noticed that she struggled to make friends and often played alone. Lucy had difficulty understanding social cues and engaging in reciprocal conversations, which made it hard for her to connect with her peers. Concerned about her social development, Jenna and Tom sought out social skills groups and play therapy.

Lucy joined a social skills group led by a skilled therapist who used role-playing and games to teach essential social skills. The group provided a safe and supportive environment for Sophia to practice interacting with others. She learned how to initiate conversations, take turns, and interpret body language and facial expressions.

As Lucy's social skills improved, so did her confidence. She began to form meaningful friendships and participate in group activities at school. Her teachers and classmates noticed her efforts, and Sophia found herself being invited to playdates and birthday parties. By fostering her social development through targeted interventions, Lucy was able to build the friendships she longed for. Her story underscores the importance of social skills training and the joy of connection for children with autism.

These stories of Liam, Emma, Jason, and Lucy are just a few examples of the many children with autism who have achieved success through dedication, support, and personalized interventions. Each child's journey is unique, reflecting their individual strengths and challenges. The common thread in these stories is the unwavering support from families, educators, and therapists who believe in the potential of every child with autism.

By sharing these testimonial success stories, we hope to inspire and encourage other families navigating the complexities of autism. With the right resources and a supportive community, children with autism can overcome obstacles, reach their milestones, and lead fulfilling lives.

Part II : Autism in Adolescents

Chapter 7

Transitioning to Adolescence

Adolescence is a pivotal period in any individual's life, marked by significant physical, emotional, and social changes. For individuals with Autism Spectrum Disorder (ASD), this transition can present unique challenges and opportunities. Understanding and supporting adolescents with autism through this period is crucial for their development and well-being.

Puberty and Developmental Changes

The onset of puberty brings a myriad of changes, both physical and hormonal, that can be overwhelming for any teenager. For adolescents with autism, these changes can be particularly confusing and distressing. It is essential for parents, caregivers, and educators to provide clear and consistent information about what to expect during puberty.

Physical changes such as growth spurts, changes in body shape, and the development of secondary sexual characteristics can be unsettling. Adolescents with autism may have heightened sensitivity to these changes due to sensory processing differences. For instance, the sensation of new hair growth or changes in skin texture can be uncomfortable. Providing sensory-friendly hygiene products and clothing can help ease some of these discomforts.

Hormonal fluctuations during puberty can also impact mood and behavior. Adolescents with autism might experience increased anxiety, irritability, or mood swings. It is important to monitor these changes closely and provide appropriate interventions. Open communication about emotions and feelings, using tools like social stories or visual aids, can help adolescents understand and manage their emotions better.

Social Challenges and Peer Relationships

One of the most significant challenges during adolescence is navigating social relationships. Peer interactions become more complex, and the pressure to conform to social norms increases. Adolescents with autism often struggle with social cues, making it difficult to form and maintain friendships.

Social skills training can be incredibly beneficial during this period. Structured programs that teach skills such as initiating conversations, understanding non-verbal cues, and managing social interactions can help adolescents build confidence and improve their social competence. Role-playing scenarios and social scripts can provide practical examples and rehearsal opportunities for real-life situations.

Bullying and social isolation are unfortunately common experiences for adolescents with autism. It is crucial to create a supportive and inclusive environment in schools and communities. Anti-bullying programs, peer mentoring, and inclusive extracurricular activities can foster a sense of belonging and reduce the risk of social isolation. Encouraging participation in interest-based clubs or groups can also help adolescents connect with peers who share similar interests.

Educational and Vocational Planning

The transition to adolescence often coincides with critical educational milestones, such as moving from middle school to high school. This transition can be particularly challenging for adolescents with autism due to changes in routine, increased academic demands, and larger, more complex school environments.

Individualized Education Plans (IEPs) should be revisited and updated to reflect the changing needs of the adolescent. Transition goals should include not only academic objectives but also social, emotional, and life skills development. Collaboration between parents, educators, and therapists is essential to ensure a holistic approach to the adolescent's education.

Vocational planning should also begin during adolescence. Early exposure to different career paths and job skills can help adolescents with autism identify their interests and strengths. Vocational training programs, internships, and job shadowing opportunities can provide valuable hands-on experience and prepare adolescents for future employment. Schools and community organizations often offer resources and programs specifically designed to support vocational development for individuals with disabilities.

Life Skills Development

Developing life skills is a critical aspect of preparing adolescents with autism for independence. Life skills encompass a wide range of activities, from personal hygiene and self-care to money management and navigating public transportation. Teaching these skills requires patience, repetition, and practical, real-world practice.

Self-care skills, such as grooming, dressing, and managing personal hygiene, can be challenging for adolescents with autism due to sensory sensitivities and motor coordination difficulties. Breaking tasks into smaller, manageable steps and using visual schedules can make these routines more manageable. Occupational therapists can provide valuable strategies and tools to support the development of self-care skills.

Money management is another essential life skill. Teaching adolescents about budgeting, saving, and making purchases can be facilitated through practical exercises, such as using a mock store setup or practicing with small amounts of money in real-life situations. Financial literacy programs tailored for individuals with disabilities can also be helpful.

Navigating public transportation is a crucial skill for fostering independence. Practice trips, accompanied by a caregiver or peer, can help adolescents become familiar with routes, schedules, and safety procedures. Many communities offer travel training programs specifically designed for individuals with disabilities, providing structured and supportive instruction.

Mental Health and Well-Being

Adolescence is a period of heightened vulnerability for mental health issues, and adolescents with autism are no exception. Anxiety, depression, and other mental health conditions are common co-occurring challenges. It is essential to prioritize mental health and provide access to appropriate support and interventions.

Cognitive-behavioral therapy (CBT) has been shown to be effective in addressing anxiety and depression in individuals with autism. Therapists with experience in working with adolescents on the spectrum can tailor CBT techniques to meet their specific needs. Additionally, mindfulness practices and relaxation techniques can help adolescents manage stress and anxiety.

Building a strong support network is crucial for the mental well-being of adolescents with autism. Encouraging connections with supportive family members, friends, and mentors can provide a sense of security and belonging. Participation in support groups or social skills groups can also offer valuable peer support and reduce feelings of isolation.

Sexuality and Relationships

Navigating sexuality and romantic relationships can be particularly complex for adolescents with autism. Clear, honest, and age-appropriate education about sexuality is essential. Topics such as consent, boundaries, and healthy relationships should be addressed explicitly.

Sexuality education programs designed for individuals with disabilities can provide structured and accessible information. These programs often use visual aids, social stories, and role-playing to convey important concepts. Open communication with trusted adults about questions and concerns related to sexuality is also important.

Transitioning to adolescence is a significant and often challenging period for individuals with autism. By providing tailored support, fostering social connections, and equipping adolescents with essential skills, we can help them navigate this transition successfully. Collaborative efforts between families, educators, therapists, and the broader community are essential in ensuring that adolescents with autism have the opportunities and resources they need to thrive during this critical stage of development.

Chapter 8

Educational and Vocational Planning

Transitioning from School to Adulthood
The transition from adolescence to adulthood is
a pivotal period for all individuals, but it poses
unique challenges for those on the autism
spectrum. During this time, educational and
vocational planning becomes essential to ensure
that individuals with autism can lead fulfilling
and independent lives. This chapter will explore
strategies for successful transitions, including
secondary education options, vocational training,
employment opportunities, and life skills
development.

Secondary Education Strategies
Secondary education plays a crucial role in
preparing adolescents with autism for adulthood.
It is important to tailor educational strategies to
meet the unique needs of each individual.
Inclusive education, where students with autism
learn alongside their neurotypical peers, has
proven to be beneficial in many cases. However,

it is vital to provide appropriate accommodations and support to ensure success.

Individualized Education Plans (IEPs):
A modified educational plan created to address the unique requirements of a student with a disability is called an IEP. For students with autism, an IEP should include goals and objectives that address academic, social, and behavioral development. It should also outline the accommodations and supports necessary for the student to succeed. Collaboration between educators, parents, and the student is essential in developing an effective IEP.

Specialized Programs:
In some cases, students with autism may benefit from specialized programs that offer a more tailored approach to their education. These programs can focus on developing specific skills, such as social communication, sensory integration, or vocational training. Specialized programs can provide a supportive environment where students can thrive and develop at their own pace.

Transition Services:

As students with autism approach the end of their secondary education, transition services become crucial. Transition planning should begin well before graduation to ensure a smooth shift from school to post-secondary education or employment. Transition services can include career counseling, job placement assistance, and training in life skills such as time management, financial literacy, and self-advocacy.

Vocational Training and Employment
Vocational training and employment opportunities are key components of the transition to adulthood for individuals with autism. These opportunities not only provide financial independence but also contribute to a sense of purpose and self-worth.

Vocational Training Programs:
Vocational training programs are designed to equip individuals with the skills needed for specific careers. These programs can be offered through schools, community colleges, or specialized training centers. For individuals with autism, vocational training should focus on developing both technical skills and soft skills,

such as communication, teamwork, and problem-solving.

Supported Employment:
Supported employment is a model that provides ongoing support to individuals with disabilities, including autism, in the workplace. This support can include job coaching, accommodations, and modifications to the work environment. Supported employment helps individuals with autism find and maintain meaningful employment, allowing them to contribute to the workforce while receiving the support they need.

Customized Employment:
Customized employment involves tailoring job roles to match the skills and interests of the individual with autism. This approach recognizes that traditional job descriptions may not always align with the strengths of individuals with autism. By customizing job roles, employers can create opportunities that leverage the unique talents of these individuals, resulting in a more inclusive and productive workforce.

Life Skills Development

Developing life skills is essential for individuals with autism to achieve independence and success in adulthood. Life skills encompass a wide range of abilities, from daily living tasks to social interactions and self-advocacy.

Daily Living Skills:
Daily living skills include tasks such as cooking, cleaning, personal hygiene, and managing finances. For individuals with autism, these skills may need to be explicitly taught and practiced. Occupational therapists and life skills coaches can provide valuable support in helping individuals develop these essential skills.

Social Skills:
In order to navigate social settings and form connections, social skills are essential. Individuals with autism often face challenges in understanding social cues and engaging in reciprocal communication. Social skills training can help individuals with autism develop strategies for initiating conversations, interpreting body language, and maintaining friendships. Group activities, role-playing, and social stories are effective methods for teaching social skills.

Self-Advocacy:
Self-advocacy is the ability to speak up for oneself and make choices regarding one's own life. Teaching self-advocacy skills empowers individuals with autism to express their needs, preferences, and goals. This includes understanding their rights, seeking support when needed, and making informed choices about their education, employment, and living arrangements.

Building a Supportive Network
A strong support network is essential for the successful transition to adulthood. This network can include family members, educators, healthcare providers, and community organizations.

Family Support:
Family members play a critical role in supporting individuals with autism throughout their transition to adulthood. They can provide emotional support, assist with decision-making, and advocate for necessary services. Encouraging independence while providing a safety net of support is a delicate balance that families must navigate.

Educational and Community Resources: Educational institutions and community organizations offer a wealth of resources for individuals with autism and their families. These resources can include transition programs, vocational training, support groups, and recreational activities. Connecting with local autism organizations can provide valuable information and opportunities for social engagement.

Healthcare and Mental Health Services: Access to healthcare and mental health services is vital for individuals with autism as they transition to adulthood. Regular medical check-ups, counseling, and therapy can help address any co-occurring conditions and support overall well-being. Healthcare providers should be knowledgeable about autism and able to provide appropriate care and referrals.

Inspiring Stories of Adolescents Overcoming Challenges

To illustrate the potential for success, this section includes testimonial success stories of adolescents with autism who have overcome challenges and achieved their goals. These stories highlight the importance of individualized support, perseverance, and the belief in one's abilities.

Emily's Trip to University

Emily had severe difficulties in her social connections and academic achievements since she was diagnosed with autism at an early age. With the help of her committed instructors and a customized IEP, she achieved academic success and excellent self-advocacy abilities. Emily had a smooth adjustment to college, where she is currently enrolled in social clubs and working toward a computer science degree.

Michael's Career Achievement

Michael found it difficult to study in conventional classroom settings, but he flourished in interactive learning settings. Through a program of vocational training, he found his love for woodworking. Michael now has a prosperous carpentry company, making custom furniture and hiring other people with disabilities, thanks to the assistance of his job coach and tailored work possibilities.

Sarah's Independent Life

Having been diagnosed with autism throughout her adolescence, Sarah struggled with day-to-day duties and social interactions. Sarah was able to learn how to cook, use public transportation, and handle her finances with the support of her family and life skills coach. She currently works part-time at a neighborhood bookstore, lives independently in her apartment, and is heavily involved in the community.

For people with autism, entering adulthood is a big milestone, and they may reach their full potential with the correct planning and support. The development of life skills, educational and career strategies, and a robust support system are crucial elements of this journey. We can assist people with autism in leading happy and meaningful lives by encouraging independence, supporting self-advocacy, and recognizing accomplishments.

Chapter 9

Testimonial Success Stories: Adolescents

Adolescence is a period of significant change and challenge for any individual, and for those on the autism spectrum, these years can bring unique hurdles as well as remarkable triumphs. In this chapter, we explore the personal stories of adolescents with autism who have navigated their teenage years with resilience, determination, and success. These testimonials not only highlight their achievements but also offer insights into the strategies and support systems that have facilitated their journeys.

The Journey of Self-Discovery: Sarah's Story

Sarah was diagnosed with autism at the age of 12, a time when she was already grappling with the complexities of middle school. Initially, Sarah and her parents felt overwhelmed by the diagnosis. They worried about her future and how she would handle the social and academic pressures of adolescence.

However, Sarah's journey turned out to be one of self-discovery and empowerment. With the support of her family, teachers, and a dedicated therapist, Sarah began to understand her unique strengths and challenges. Her parents made it a priority to educate themselves about autism, attending workshops and joining support groups to better advocate for their daughter.

One of the pivotal moments in Sarah's journey was her involvement in a social skills group specifically designed for adolescents with autism. Here, she learned practical strategies for navigating social interactions, managing anxiety, and building friendships. These skills not only helped her in her day-to-day life but also boosted her confidence.

Sarah also discovered a passion for art. Encouraged by her art teacher, she began to express herself through painting and drawing. This creative outlet became a source of joy and a way for her to communicate her emotions and experiences. Sarah's artwork gained recognition, and she was invited to showcase her pieces in local galleries. This not only validated her talent but also provided her with a sense of accomplishment and purpose.

Today, Sarah is a thriving high school student who continues to pursue her passion for art. She has a close-knit group of friends and actively participates in school activities. Her story is a testament to the power of self-discovery, supportive environments, and the importance of nurturing individual strengths.

Overcoming Academic Challenges: Michael's Story

Michael was always a bright student, but his autism made certain aspects of school life particularly challenging. He struggled with sensory sensitivities, which made the noisy and bustling environment of his middle school overwhelming. Additionally, he found it difficult to organize his thoughts and manage his time effectively, often leading to frustration and anxiety.

Recognizing these challenges, Michael's parents worked closely with his school to develop an

Individualized Education Plan (IEP) tailored to his needs. This plan included accommodations such as a quieter workspace, extended time for tests, and the use of assistive technology to help with organization and note-taking.

One of the most effective strategies for Michael was the introduction of a mentor. This mentor, an older student with experience in managing similar challenges, provided Michael with guidance, support, and practical tips for navigating school life. They met regularly to discuss strategies for handling assignments, managing sensory overload, and coping with social situations.

Michael also benefited from participating in extracurricular activities that aligned with his interests. He joined the school's robotics club, where he found a supportive community and an outlet for his problem-solving skills. The hands-on nature of robotics allowed him to apply his knowledge in a practical and engaging way, boosting his confidence and fostering a sense of belonging.

Through these combined efforts, Michael not only improved academically but also developed valuable life skills. He learned how to advocate for himself, utilize available resources, and build a network of support. By the time he reached high school, Michael was thriving both academically and socially. He is now considering a future in engineering, inspired by his experiences in the robotics club.

Building Social Connections: Matilda's Story

For Matilda, social interactions were always a source of anxiety and confusion. Diagnosed with autism at a young age, she often felt isolated and struggled to form meaningful connections with her peers. Her parents were concerned about her emotional well-being and sought ways to help her build social skills and confidence.

Matilda's breakthrough came when she joined a drama club for students with special needs. Initially hesitant, she soon discovered that the structured nature of theater provided a safe space for her to explore social interactions and express herself. The club's inclusive and supportive environment allowed Matilda to practice social cues, teamwork, and communication in a way that felt manageable and enjoyable.

Through drama, Matilda found her voice. She developed close friendships with other club members, who shared similar experiences and understood her challenges. These relationships extended beyond the drama club, providing her with a supportive peer group both in and out of school.

Matilda's parents also played a crucial role in her social development. They encouraged her to participate in community activities and facilitated playdates with peers from the drama club. They also worked with a social skills coach, who provided Matilda with targeted strategies for initiating conversations, maintaining friendships, and handling social conflicts.

As Matilda's confidence grew, so did her willingness to engage in new experiences. She joined other school clubs and activities, expanding her social circle and discovering new interests. Today, Matilda is a confident and outgoing teenager who enjoys performing and actively participates in her school community.

Embracing Individuality: Alex's Story
Alex's story is one of embracing individuality and finding strength in his unique perspective. Diagnosed with autism at the age of 14, Alex initially struggled with the stigma and misunderstandings associated with his diagnosis. He felt different from his peers and often worried about fitting in.

However, with the support of his family and a dedicated group of educators, Alex began to see his autism as a part of his identity rather than a limitation. His parents emphasized the importance of self-acceptance and encouraged him to pursue his interests and passions.

Technology was an interest of Alex's. He was naturally good with computers, and he spent hours learning how to program and playing with new applications. His parents saw this talent and signed him up for a coding camp, where he flourished and made friends with other tech enthusiasts.

Alex's engagement with technology gave him a sense of direction and opened doors to new prospects. In addition to joining online groups and taking part in hackathons, he also launched a tech blog where he discussed his ideas and projects. Through these encounters, Alex discovered a community that appreciated his abilities and viewpoint and developed a strong sense of self-worth.

Alex is a high school student currently aspiring to work in technology. He is pleased with his original contributions and has faith in his skills. His narrative emphasizes the value of valuing uniqueness and discovering one's passions as sources of strength.

These testimonies bear witness to the tenacity and promise of young autistic people. Every narrative highlights the value of cultivating unique skills, individualized approaches, and encouraging surroundings. We hope that by sharing these journeys, we will encourage and help those who are walking similar routes with useful insights. Through overcoming scholastic obstacles, forming social relationships, or finding their passion, these teenagers show that, given the correct assistance, they are capable of thriving and achieving extraordinary success.

Part III: Autism in Adults

Chapter 10

Adult Diagnosis and Self-Identification

Autism Spectrum Disorder (ASD) is often associated with children, but many adults live their entire lives without an official diagnosis. For these individuals, understanding their autism in adulthood can be both a relief and a challenge. This chapter explores the journey of adult diagnosis, the impact it has on self-identity, and the strategies for self-advocacy and acceptance.

The Journey to Diagnosis
Many adults who seek an autism diagnosis have spent years feeling different but not knowing why. They might have struggled with social interactions, sensory sensitivities, or maintaining employment, often attributing their challenges to other factors like anxiety or depression. It is not uncommon for these individuals to reach adulthood without a diagnosis due to a lack of

awareness about autism during their childhood
or misdiagnosis by healthcare professionals.

The journey to diagnosis often begins with a
moment of realization or a triggering event. This
could be reading about autism and recognizing
oneself in the descriptions, a family member
receiving a diagnosis that prompts self-reflection,
or encountering difficulties that lead to seeking
professional help. For many, the decision to
pursue a diagnosis is driven by a desire for
understanding and validation of their
experiences.

The Diagnostic Process
Getting an autism diagnosis as an adult involves
several steps and can vary depending on the
healthcare system and availability of specialists.
Typically, the process includes:

Initial Assessment: The journey often starts with
a visit to a general practitioner or mental health
professional who can refer the individual to a
specialist. The initial assessment may involve
discussing symptoms, personal history, and
reasons for seeking a diagnosis.

Comprehensive Evaluation: A thorough evaluation is conducted by a specialist, such as a psychologist or psychiatrist with experience in adult autism. This evaluation includes interviews, questionnaires, and observations to assess behaviors and experiences consistent with autism. The specialist may also gather information from family members or close friends to provide additional context.

Diagnostic Criteria: The diagnosis is based on criteria outlined in the Diagnostic and Statistical Manual of Mental Disorders (DSM-5) or the International Classification of Diseases (ICD-11). The specialist looks for persistent deficits in social communication and interaction, as well as restricted and repetitive behaviors or interests.

Feedback and Diagnosis: After the evaluation, the specialist provides feedback and confirms whether the criteria for ASD are met. This moment can be a turning point, offering clarity and a sense of relief for many individuals who have long sought an explanation for their experiences.

The Impact of Diagnosis

Receiving an autism diagnosis in adulthood can have profound effects on self-identity and mental well-being. For many, it provides a framework for understanding past experiences and behaviors. The diagnosis can validate feelings of being different and offer a sense of belonging to a community with shared experiences.

Relief and Validation: One of the most immediate reactions to a diagnosis is often relief. Many adults feel a sense of validation, as the diagnosis confirms that their challenges have a name and a cause. It can be comforting to know that they are not alone and that others have similar experiences.

Reframing Past Experiences: With the diagnosis, individuals can reframe their past experiences through the lens of autism. Behaviors that were previously misunderstood or criticized by others can now be seen as part of their autistic traits. This reframing can lead to greater self-compassion and a reduction in self-blame.

Emotional Responses: Alongside relief, there can be complex emotional responses, including grief for missed opportunities or regret for not having known sooner. Some individuals may feel anger towards a system that failed to recognize their needs or provide appropriate support. It's important to acknowledge and process these emotions as part of the journey.

Self-Advocacy and Acceptance
Self-advocacy and acceptance are crucial components of living well with an autism diagnosis. They involve understanding one's own needs, communicating effectively, and fostering a positive self-image.

Understanding Needs: Knowing one's strengths and challenges is essential for effective self-advocacy. Adults with autism often benefit from creating personalized strategies to manage sensory sensitivities, social interactions, and executive functioning tasks. This might include using sensory tools, establishing routines, or seeking accommodations in the workplace.

Effective Communication: Being able to communicate one's needs and preferences is a key aspect of self-advocacy. This includes educating others about autism and how it affects the individual. For some, this might mean disclosing their diagnosis to employers, colleagues, or friends to facilitate understanding and support.

Building a Support Network: A strong support network can make a significant difference in navigating life with autism. This network might include family, friends, healthcare professionals, and autism support groups. Making connections with people who have gone through similar things to you can offer a feeling of community, practical guidance, and emotional support.

Embracing Identity: Acceptance involves embracing one's identity as an autistic person. This means recognizing that autism is an integral part of who they are and not something to be ashamed of. Embracing this identity can lead to greater self-confidence and a more authentic life.

The Role of Therapy and Counseling
Therapy and counseling can be valuable tools for adults with autism, both in coming to terms with the diagnosis and in developing coping strategies. Therapists with experience in autism can provide support in several areas:

Cognitive Behavioral Therapy (CBT): CBT can help individuals manage anxiety, depression, and other co-occurring conditions. It focuses on identifying and changing negative thought patterns and behaviors.

Social Skills Training: Therapy can include training to improve social interactions, understand social cues, and develop meaningful relationships.

Occupational Therapy: Occupational therapists can assist with sensory processing issues, daily living skills, and workplace accommodations.

Counseling: Individual or group counseling provides a safe space to explore feelings about the diagnosis, process past experiences, and develop self-advocacy skills.

Being diagnosed with autism in adulthood can be a life-changing event that provides insight and a way forward for more acceptance and self-awareness. The path to a diagnosis and beyond can be difficult, but it also presents chances for personal development, self-advocacy, and creating a network of support. Living a full and genuine life can be achieved by accepting one's autism identity.

Chapter 11

Independent Living and Support

For adults with Autism Spectrum Disorder (ASD), achieving independent living is a critical milestone. Independence means different things to different individuals; it can range from managing personal care and finances to living in one's own home or pursuing meaningful employment. This chapter explores the various aspects of independent living, offering strategies and support systems that can help individuals with autism lead fulfilling lives.

Housing and Living Arrangements
Choosing the right living arrangement is essential for fostering independence. There are several options available, each with its own set of advantages and challenges.

Living with Family

Many adults with autism continue to live with their families, benefiting from the familiarity and support this environment provides. Families can create structured routines and safe spaces that accommodate sensory needs. However, it's important to plan for the future, considering what will happen when parents or primary caregivers are no longer able to provide support.

Supported Living

Supported living arrangements offer a balance between independence and assistance. These can include shared housing with on-site support staff or individual apartments with visiting aides. Supported living programs are tailored to meet the specific needs of the individual, providing help with daily tasks, medical care, and social activities. This option allows adults with autism to experience greater independence while still having access to necessary support.

Independent Living

Some adults with autism achieve full independence, living alone or with roommates. This option requires a high level of self-sufficiency, including the ability to manage finances, perform household chores, and navigate social situations. Independent living is often the result of gradual skill development and a strong support network.

Financial Management and Employment
Financial independence is a significant aspect of adult life. Managing money, budgeting, and employment are key components.

Budgeting and Financial Skills

Teaching financial skills is crucial. This includes understanding how to budget, save, and spend money wisely. Financial literacy programs and one-on-one coaching can be beneficial. Many individuals with autism benefit from using visual aids and technology to manage their finances, such as budgeting apps and online banking tools.

Employment Opportunities

Employment provides both financial independence and a sense of purpose. Finding the right job can be challenging, but many individuals with autism excel in roles that match their skills and interests. It's important to consider job environments that are supportive and accommodating. Some common fields where adults with autism thrive include technology, art, and detail-oriented tasks.

Supported Employment Programs

Supported employment programs offer job training, placement, and ongoing support. These programs work with employers to create inclusive workplaces and provide job coaches who assist individuals with autism in their roles. Supported employment increases job retention and satisfaction by addressing the unique needs of the individual.

Navigating Healthcare and Services
Access to healthcare and services is essential for maintaining overall well-being. Adults with autism often require specialized healthcare that addresses both physical and mental health needs.

Healthcare Providers

Finding healthcare providers who understand autism is crucial. This includes general practitioners, mental health professionals, and specialists who are experienced in treating adults with autism. Regular check-ups, preventive care, and mental health support are all important components of a comprehensive healthcare plan.

Mental Health Support

Many adults with autism experience co-occurring mental health conditions such as anxiety, depression, or obsessive-compulsive disorder. Access to mental health services, including therapy and medication management, can significantly improve quality of life. Therapies such as Cognitive Behavioral Therapy (CBT) are often effective in addressing these conditions.

Community Services and Resources

Community-based services offer additional support. These can include social skills groups, recreational activities, and life skills training. Local autism organizations and advocacy groups often provide resources and information on available services. Utilizing community resources helps individuals with autism build social networks and develop important life skills.

Developing Life Skills

Life skills are essential for independent living. These skills encompass a wide range of daily activities, from personal care to managing relationships.

Personal Care and Hygiene

Teaching personal care skills is foundational. This includes grooming, dressing, and maintaining hygiene. Visual schedules, checklists, and step-by-step instructions can be helpful tools. Consistent routines and positive reinforcement encourage independence in these areas.

Cooking and Nutrition

Learning to prepare meals and make healthy food choices is another critical life skill. Cooking classes designed for individuals with autism can teach basic culinary skills. Additionally, understanding nutrition and how to plan balanced meals promotes overall health.

Time Management and Organization

Effective time management and organizational skills are necessary for managing daily tasks and responsibilities. Tools such as planners, calendars, and reminder apps can help individuals with autism stay organized and on track. These tools also assist in managing appointments, work schedules, and social activities.

Building Social Connections
Social connections are vital for emotional well-being and a sense of community.

Developing Social Skills

Autism sufferers who receive social skills training can better navigate social situations. This includes understanding social cues, building conversation skills, and developing empathy. Role-playing, social stories, and group activities are effective methods for teaching these skills.

Forming Friendships and Relationships

Building and maintaining friendships and romantic relationships can be challenging but rewarding. Encouraging participation in social groups, clubs, or interest-based activities helps individuals with autism meet others with similar interests. Support from family and friends is also crucial in fostering these relationships.

Community Involvement

Engaging in community activities provides opportunities for socialization and personal growth. Volunteering, attending local events, and participating in recreational activities contribute to a sense of belonging. Community involvement also helps individuals with autism develop new skills and interests.

Achieving independent living is a multifaceted journey for adults with autism. With the right support and resources, individuals can develop the skills needed to lead fulfilling and independent lives. Whether through supported living arrangements, employment opportunities, or community involvement, the path to independence is unique for each person. By focusing on strengths and addressing challenges, adults with autism can thrive in their pursuit of independence.

Chapter 12

Relationships and Social Integration

Relationships and social integration are main aspects of human life, contributing significantly to overall well-being and quality of life. For adults with autism, forming and maintaining relationships can be challenging due to difficulties with social communication and interaction. However, with the right support and strategies, meaningful relationships and social inclusion are entirely achievable.

Romantic Relationships

Romantic relationships can be particularly challenging for adults with autism, but they are just as rewarding and fulfilling as they are for neurotypical individuals. People with autism often experience the same desires for love, companionship, and intimacy.

1. **Understanding and Communication**
   One of the key challenges in romantic relationships for adults with autism is

understanding and communicating feelings. Individuals on the spectrum may struggle with reading social cues, understanding nuanced emotional expressions, or expressing their own emotions clearly. Effective communication strategies, such as using clear and direct language, can help bridge these gaps. Partners can benefit from learning about autism and adopting patience and empathy in their interactions.

2. **Navigating Dating**

   The dating process can be daunting. Structured approaches, such as dating websites or apps that cater to individuals with autism, can provide a safer and more controlled environment for meeting potential partners. Social skills training and role-playing scenarios can also help adults with autism prepare for dates and feel more confident.

3. **Maintaining Relationships**

   Sustaining a romantic relationship involves ongoing effort and adaptation. Regular and open communication, establishing routines, and setting clear expectations can help. Partners should work together to find balance and understand each other's needs, including sensory sensitivities or social preferences.

Friendships and Social Networks

Friendships provide emotional support, companionship, and opportunities for shared activities. For adults with autism, forming and maintaining friendships can be challenging but rewarding.

1. **Finding Like-Minded Individuals**
   Finding friends with similar interests can make social interactions more comfortable and enjoyable. Joining clubs, groups, or online communities focused on specific hobbies can provide opportunities to meet like-minded individuals. Local autism support groups or social skills groups can also be valuable resources.
2. **Building Social Skills**
   Social skills training can help adults with autism navigate social interactions more effectively. This training often includes understanding body language, practicing

conversation skills, and learning how to initiate and maintain social connections. Role-playing and real-life practice are essential components of this training.

3. **Sustaining Friendships**

   Maintaining friendships requires effort and understanding from both parties. Regular communication, whether through messages, calls, or in-person meetups, helps keep the connection strong. Being aware of each other's boundaries and preferences, especially regarding sensory sensitivities or social fatigue, can enhance the quality of the friendship.

Community Involvement and Hobbies

Being part of a community and engaging in hobbies can significantly enhance social integration and personal fulfillment.

1. **Community Engagement**

   Involvement in community activities, such as volunteering, attending local events, or participating in religious or cultural groups, can provide a sense of belonging. These activities offer opportunities to meet new people, develop new skills, and contribute to the community.

2. **Pursuing Hobbies**

   Hobbies provide a valuable outlet for creativity, relaxation, and social interaction. Whether it's art, music, sports, or gaming, hobbies can connect individuals with others who share their passions. For adults with autism, structured activities with clear rules and expectations can be particularly appealing.

Overcoming Social Isolation

Social isolation is a significant concern for many adults with autism. It can lead to feelings of loneliness, depression, and anxiety. Addressing social isolation requires proactive steps and supportive interventions.

1. **Creating Support Networks**

   Developing a strong support network of family, friends, and professionals is crucial. Regular check-ins, social events, and supportive conversations can help reduce feelings of isolation. Support groups, both in-person and online, offer a safe space for sharing experiences and gaining encouragement from others facing similar challenges.

2. **Utilizing Technology**

   Technology can be a powerful tool for social connection. Social media, online forums, and virtual meetups provide platforms for communication and social interaction. However, it is important to use these tools wisely to avoid potential pitfalls such as cyberbullying or over-reliance on virtual interactions.

3. **Therapeutic Support**

   Therapy can help address social anxiety and other barriers to social integration. Cognitive-behavioral therapy (CBT) and social skills training are particularly effective. Therapists can work with individuals to develop strategies for managing social situations, reducing anxiety, and building confidence.

Case Study: David's Journey to Social Integration

David, a 30-year-old adult with autism, struggled with social isolation for many years. His difficulties with social communication and sensory sensitivities made it hard for him to form and maintain relationships. However, with support and determination, David made significant strides toward social integration.

1. **Finding His Community**
   David started by joining a local autism support group, where he met others who understood his experiences. This group provided a safe and supportive environment for him to practice social skills and gain confidence.

2. **Pursuing Interests**
   David had a passion for photography, which he pursued as a hobby. He joined a photography club, where he connected with individuals who shared his interest. This common ground made it easier for him to initiate conversations and build friendships.

3. **Building Relationships**
   Through the support group and photography club, David developed meaningful friendships. He learned to communicate more effectively and to manage his sensory sensitivities in social settings. Over time, he felt less isolated and more connected to his community.

4. **Romantic Relationship**
   Eventually, Alex met his partner through a mutual friend. They took the time to understand each other's needs and developed a strong, supportive relationship. David's partner's patience and understanding played a crucial role in helping him navigate the complexities of a romantic relationship.

Social integration is a multifaceted journey for adults with autism, encompassing romantic relationships, friendships, community involvement, and overcoming isolation. With the right support, strategies, and understanding, adults with autism can build fulfilling and meaningful social connections. David's story is just one example of how determination, support, and finding the right community can lead to a richer, more connected life.

Chapter 13

Testimonial Success Stories: Adults

Navigating adulthood with autism presents unique challenges and opportunities. This chapter shares inspiring stories of adults who have embraced their autism and found success, fulfillment, and happiness. Their journeys demonstrate the importance of self-advocacy, supportive environments, and recognizing individual strengths.

Embracing Late Diagnosis: Maria's Journey
Maria's story begins with a late diagnosis. At 32, after years of feeling different and struggling with social interactions, Maria sought help. A diagnosis of autism spectrum disorder (ASD) brought relief and a new understanding of herself.

"I always felt like I was swimming against the tide," Maria shares. "The diagnosis was a turning point. It provided me with a structure to make sense of my experiences."

Maria's journey highlights the transformative power of understanding and acceptance. Post-diagnosis, she engaged in therapy, joined support groups, and began to advocate for herself at work. She learned to communicate her needs effectively, leading to better relationships with colleagues and a more accommodating work environment.

"I've learned to embrace my unique way of thinking," Maria says. "It's a different viewpoint, not a deficit.
."

Maria's career flourished once she could leverage her strengths—attention to detail, analytical skills, and deep focus. Today, she works as a data analyst, a role that perfectly suits her abilities. Her story underscores the importance of recognizing and valuing neurodiversity in the workplace.

Finding Independence: James' Path to Self-Sufficiency

James, diagnosed with autism at age 5, faced significant challenges in his early years. Social interactions were particularly difficult, and he struggled in traditional educational settings. However, with a supportive family and specialized educational programs, James gradually found his path.

"I used to believe that I was incapable of being self-sufficient," James recalls. "But my family and mentors always believed in me."

James' transition to adulthood involved vocational training that focused on his interests and strengths. He developed skills in computer programming, an area where he excelled. With the guidance of a job coach, James secured a position at a tech company known for its inclusive hiring practices.

Living independently was James' next milestone. He moved into a supported living arrangement, which provided the right balance of autonomy and assistance. Over time, he gained confidence in managing daily tasks, from cooking to budgeting.

"Independence doesn't mean doing everything alone," James explains. "It's about knowing when to reach out for help and finding systems which work for you."

James' journey illustrates the importance of tailored support and the belief that individuals with autism can lead fulfilling, independent lives.

Advocacy and Empowerment: Sarah's Mission Sarah's experience with autism inspired her to become an advocate and educator. Diagnosed as a teenager, she faced bullying and misunderstanding. Her determination to change the narrative around autism led her to a career in advocacy.

"I wanted no one else to experience what I had," says Sarah. "Education is key to creating a more inclusive society."

Sarah founded a non-profit organization dedicated to autism awareness and support. Through workshops, seminars, and online resources, her organization educates the public about autism, promotes acceptance, and provides practical support to individuals and families.

One of Sarah's initiatives is a mentorship program that pairs young adults with autism with mentors who have navigated similar challenges. This program has been transformative, offering guidance, friendship, and real-life role models.

"Seeing the impact of our work is incredibly rewarding," Sarah says. "Every success story is a reminder of why we do this."

Sarah's advocacy extends to policy work. She collaborates with legislators to promote laws that support the rights and needs of autistic individuals. Her efforts have led to increased funding for autism services and better protections in the workplace.

Thriving in Creative Fields: David's Artistic Expression
David's story is one of discovering and nurturing talent. Diagnosed with autism at a young age, David often found solace in art. Drawing and

painting became his preferred modes of communication, allowing him to express emotions and ideas that were difficult to convey verbally.

"Art is my language," David explains. "It's how I make sense of the world."

Supported by his family and teachers, David pursued his passion. He attended a specialized art school where he honed his skills and developed a unique artistic style. His work, characterized by vivid colors and intricate details, began to attract attention.

David's first gallery show was a turning point. It provided a platform to share his perspective and challenge stereotypes about autism. His art speaks to the complexities of the autistic experience, offering viewers a glimpse into his world.

"Art has given me a voice," David says. "It's also connected me with a community that values and supports my work."

Today, David is a successful artist with exhibitions across the country. His journey highlights the importance of supporting autistic individuals in pursuing their passions and the potential for creative expression to foster connection and understanding.

Building Inclusive Communities: Mark's Leadership

Mark's experience with autism led him to become a community leader. Diagnosed in his twenties, Mark faced challenges in social interactions and employment. However, he also recognized the importance of community and support networks.

"I wanted to create spaces where everyone feels welcome and valued," Mark shares.

Mark founded an inclusive community center that offers a variety of programs, from social clubs to skill-building workshops. The center serves as a hub for autistic individuals and their families, providing a place to connect, learn, and grow.

"Our goal is to celebrate neurodiversity and promote inclusion," Mark explains. "We believe in the strengths and potential of every individual."

Mark's leadership has fostered a strong, supportive community. The center's programs help members build confidence, develop skills, and form meaningful relationships. Through his work, Mark has created a model for inclusive community-building that others are beginning to replicate.

Part IV:

Cross-Age Insights and Strategies

Part IV: Cross-Age Insights and Strategies

Chapter 14

Sensory Processing and Regulation

Understanding Sensory Needs

Sensory processing is a critical aspect of understanding autism. Many individuals on the autism spectrum experience sensory processing differences, which can affect how they perceive and respond to sensory stimuli. These differences can lead to sensory overload, discomfort, and difficulties in everyday functioning. Understanding sensory needs and implementing effective regulation strategies are essential for supporting individuals with autism.

Sensory processing refers to the way the nervous system receives, organizes, and interprets sensory information from the environment and the body. This information includes inputs from the five traditional senses (sight, sound, touch, taste, and smell) as well as proprioception (sense of body position) and vestibular (sense of balance) systems. Individuals with autism may have hyper-sensitive (over-responsive) or hypo-sensitive (under-responsive) reactions to these sensory inputs.

Common Sensory Processing Challenges
Individuals with autism may exhibit a range of sensory processing challenges, which can vary widely in severity and type. Common sensory processing challenges include:

Auditory Sensitivity: Many individuals with autism are sensitive to certain sounds, which can be overwhelming or even painful. Everyday noises such as vacuum cleaners, sirens, or crowded environments can cause distress and lead to avoidance behaviors or meltdowns.

Visual Sensitivity: Bright lights, fluorescent lighting, or fast-moving visual stimuli can be overwhelming. Some individuals may be sensitive to specific colors or patterns, while others might find it difficult to filter out visual distractions.

Tactile Sensitivity: Some individuals with autism are hypersensitive to touch. Clothing tags, certain fabrics, or unexpected touch can cause significant discomfort. Conversely, some may seek out deep pressure or certain textures for comfort and sensory regulation.

Oral Sensitivity: Sensitivity to certain tastes, textures, or temperatures can affect eating habits. Individuals may have strong preferences or aversions to specific foods, which can lead to restricted diets and nutritional challenges.

Proprioceptive and Vestibular Sensitivity: Difficulties with body awareness and balance are common. Individuals may seek out activities that provide proprioceptive input, such as jumping or crashing into objects, or they may have a strong need for movement to feel regulated.

Strategies for Sensory Regulation
Effective sensory regulation strategies can help individuals with autism manage sensory processing challenges and improve their overall well-being. These strategies should be

personalized to meet the unique sensory needs of each individual.

Creating a Sensory-Friendly Environment: Modifying the environment to reduce sensory stressors can be beneficial. This may include using noise-canceling headphones, adjusting lighting, providing sensory-friendly spaces, and minimizing clutter and visual distractions.

Sensory Diets: A sensory diet is a personalized plan that incorporates specific sensory activities throughout the day to help regulate sensory input. Activities may include swinging, jumping on a trampoline, using weighted blankets, or engaging in deep pressure activities. Occupational therapists can help design and implement sensory diets.

Visual Supports and Communication Tools: Using visual supports, such as picture schedules, social stories, and visual timers, can help individuals anticipate and understand sensory experiences. These tools can provide a sense of control and predictability.

Mindfulness and Relaxation Techniques: Mindfulness exercises, such as deep breathing, progressive muscle relaxation, and guided imagery, can help individuals manage sensory overload and reduce anxiety. Teaching these techniques can empower individuals to self-regulate.

Occupational Therapy: Occupational therapists specialize in sensory integration therapy, which aims to improve the brain's ability to process and respond to sensory input. Therapy sessions often involve playful, sensory-rich activities that are designed to challenge and support sensory processing skills.

Adaptive Equipment and Assistive Technology: Tools such as fidget toys, weighted vests, and adaptive seating can provide sensory input that helps with regulation. Assistive technology, including apps and devices, can also support sensory processing and communication needs.

Case Studies and Success Stories

To illustrate the impact of effective sensory regulation strategies, here are a few success stories from individuals with autism:

Case Study 1: Jake's Journey to Sensory Regulation

Jake, a 10-year-old boy with autism, struggled with auditory and tactile sensitivities. Loud noises, such as school bells and crowded cafeterias, often triggered meltdowns, while certain clothing fabrics caused extreme discomfort. His occupational therapist introduced a sensory diet that included noise-canceling headphones, deep pressure activities, and the use of soft, seamless clothing. Over time, Jake learned to recognize his sensory triggers and use self-regulation strategies. He began to participate more fully in school activities and social interactions, demonstrating remarkable progress in managing his sensory challenges.

Case Study 2: Emma's Empowerment Through Sensory Tools

Emma, a 25-year-old woman with autism, faced significant challenges with proprioceptive and vestibular processing. She often felt ungrounded and sought out intense movement to feel regulated. Her occupational therapist introduced a variety of sensory tools, including a weighted blanket, a balance board, and structured physical activities such as yoga and dance. These tools helped Emma develop better body awareness and improve her balance. She gained confidence in her daily activities and even joined a local dance group, where she found a supportive community and an outlet for her sensory needs.

Case Study 3: Lucas' Transformation with Visual Supports

Lucas, a 15-year-old teenager with autism, had difficulties with transitions and sensory overload in new environments. His family and teachers implemented visual supports, such as a visual schedule and social stories, to prepare him for changes and new experiences. These tools provided Lucas with a sense of predictability and control, reducing his anxiety. As a result, Lucas became more willing to try new activities and navigate unfamiliar settings. His improved self-regulation skills enabled him to participate in a school trip to a busy science museum, where he enjoyed the exhibits without feeling overwhelmed.

Understanding and addressing sensory processing needs is a crucial aspect of supporting individuals with autism. By recognizing the unique sensory profiles of each person and implementing tailored strategies, caregivers, educators, and therapists can help individuals with autism achieve better sensory regulation and overall well-being. Sensory processing is not just about managing challenges; it is about empowering individuals to thrive and fully participate in their environments.

New methods and resources will become available as knowledge about sensory processing expands, providing even more chances for people with autism to live happy, purposeful lives. The triumphant tales of Jake, Emma, and Lucas underscore the revolutionary influence of efficacious ways for regulating sensory input, proving that persons with autism can surmount sensory obstacles and realize their complete potential when provided with appropriate assistance.

Chapter 15

Communication Techniques and Tools

Effective communication is fundamental to human interaction, yet for individuals on the autism spectrum, it can present unique challenges. Communication difficulties are a core characteristic of Autism Spectrum Disorder (ASD), ranging from nonverbal individuals to those who struggle with pragmatic language skills. This chapter explores various communication techniques and tools designed to support individuals with autism in expressing themselves and understanding others.

Understanding Communication Challenges in Autism
Communication in autism can be affected in several ways:

Verbal Communication: Some individuals may have limited or no spoken language, while others might have extensive vocabularies but struggle with conversational skills.

Nonverbal Communication: Difficulties in understanding and using gestures, facial expressions, and body language are common. Social Communication: Challenges in understanding social cues, taking turns in conversation, and maintaining the flow of dialogue.

These challenges can lead to frustration, social isolation, and misunderstandings. However, with the right support and tools, individuals with autism can enhance their communication abilities and engage more effectively with those around them.

Augmentative and Alternative Communication (AAC)

AAC encompasses a range of communication methods used to supplement or replace speech. These tools are particularly beneficial for nonverbal individuals or those with limited verbal abilities.

Low-Tech AAC:

Picture Exchange Communication System (PECS): PECS is a widely used system where individuals use pictures to communicate their needs and desires. It involves teaching the individual to exchange a picture for a desired item or activity, gradually building more complex communication.

Communication Boards: These boards display symbols, pictures, or words that the individual can point to in order to communicate. They can be customized to include relevant vocabulary for the user's daily life.

High-Tech AAC:

Speech-Generating Devices (SGDs): These electronic devices produce spoken language. Users can select words, phrases, or sentences on a screen, and the device vocalizes the selections. Modern SGDs often come with customizable software that can grow with the user's needs.

Mobile Apps: There are numerous apps available for tablets and smartphones that function as AAC tools. These apps often include features such as symbol-based communication, text-to-speech, and predictive text.

Social Communication Strategies

Beyond AAC, there are several strategies to support social communication skills:

Social Stories:

Developed by Carol Gray, social stories are short, descriptive narratives that explain social situations and appropriate responses. They can help individuals with autism understand social cues, routines, and expectations. Social stories are personalized and often use simple language and visual aids to enhance comprehension.
Comic Strip Conversations:

This technique involves drawing conversations in comic strip format to illustrate social interactions and highlight thoughts and feelings. It helps individuals understand perspectives, intentions, and emotions in social contexts.
Role-Playing:

Practicing social scenarios through role-playing can help individuals with autism prepare for real-life interactions. This method allows them to rehearse appropriate responses, learn turn-taking, and develop conversational skills in a supportive environment.
Enhancing Pragmatic Language Skills
Pragmatic language refers to the use of language in social contexts, including understanding and using conversational rules. Many individuals with

autism struggle with pragmatic language, which can impact their social interactions.

Explicit Teaching of Social Rules:

Teaching the rules of conversation explicitly, such as taking turns, staying on topic, and using appropriate greetings and farewells, can be beneficial. Visual supports and social stories can aid in this teaching process.

Video Modeling:

Video modeling involves showing videos of appropriate social interactions. Individuals can watch and learn from these examples, which can be more engaging and relatable than verbal instructions alone.

Peer-Mediated Interventions:

Encouraging interactions with neurotypical peers in structured settings can provide opportunities for practicing social communication. Peers can model appropriate behaviors and offer feedback in a naturalistic environment.

Supporting Communication in Various Settings

Effective communication support extends across different settings, including home, school, and community environments.

Home:

Consistency is key. Using the same communication tools and strategies at home as in other settings reinforces learning. Family members should be trained in the use of AAC devices and strategies to ensure consistent support.
School:

Collaboration between educators, speech-language pathologists, and parents is crucial. Individualized Education Plans (IEPs) should include communication goals and outline specific supports, such as the use of AAC devices in the classroom and social skills training.
Community:

Community programs and organizations can play a vital role in supporting communication. Activities such as social skills groups, clubs, and recreational programs provide opportunities for practicing communication in a variety of social contexts.

Technology and Innovation

Advancements in technology continue to open new avenues for supporting communication in individuals with autism.

Wearable Technology:

Wearable devices, such as smartwatches and bracelets, can provide prompts and reminders for social interactions and communication. These devices can also track physiological data, helping to identify stressors that might impact communication.

Virtual Reality (VR):

VR can simulate social situations in a controlled environment, allowing individuals to practice and refine their communication skills without the pressure of real-life consequences. VR programs can be tailored to specific needs, providing a safe space for learning and growth.

Artificial Intelligence (AI):

AI-powered tools are being developed to assist with communication. For example, AI can help predict and suggest appropriate responses in conversations, offering real-time support to individuals with autism.

Effective communication is a cornerstone of personal development and social integration for individuals with autism. By leveraging a variety of communication techniques and tools, we can empower individuals on the spectrum to express themselves, connect with others, and navigate the complexities of social interactions. Ongoing research and technological advancements promise even greater support in the future, fostering a more inclusive and understanding society for all.

Chapter 16

Mental Health and Well-Being

Common Co-occurring Conditions
Autism Spectrum Disorder (ASD) often co-occurs with a variety of other mental health conditions, making it crucial to address these overlapping challenges to ensure the well-being of individuals on the spectrum. Understanding these co-occurring conditions can provide a more comprehensive approach to care and support.

Anxiety Disorders

Anxiety is one of the most common co-occurring conditions in individuals with ASD. Studies suggest that up to 40% of people on the autism spectrum also have significant anxiety issues. These can manifest as generalized anxiety disorder, social anxiety disorder, or specific phobias. The heightened sensory sensitivities and difficulties in social communication that often accompany autism can exacerbate feelings of anxiety. For instance, social situations may become overwhelming, leading to increased stress and avoidance behaviors.

Depression

Depression is another prevalent condition among those with ASD, with research indicating that about 30% of individuals on the spectrum experience depressive symptoms. The social isolation and communication challenges inherent in autism can contribute to feelings of sadness and hopelessness. Additionally, the struggle to meet societal expectations and navigate daily life can lead to chronic stress and, eventually, depression.

Attention Deficit Hyperactivity Disorder (ADHD)

ADHD is commonly diagnosed alongside autism, with studies showing a co-occurrence rate of around 28-44%. The overlapping symptoms, such as difficulties with attention, hyperactivity, and impulsivity, can complicate the diagnosis and treatment of both conditions. Individuals with both ADHD and ASD may face greater challenges in academic and social settings, requiring tailored strategies to manage their symptoms effectively.

Obsessive-Compulsive Disorder (OCD)

OCD is characterized by intrusive thoughts and repetitive behaviors, which can be particularly challenging for individuals with autism. The rigid routines and specific interests often associated with ASD can overlap with OCD symptoms, making it difficult to distinguish between the two conditions. It is essential to address these behaviors through appropriate therapeutic interventions to reduce distress and improve quality of life.

Sleep Disorders

Sleep disturbances are common in individuals with ASD, with many experiencing difficulties such as insomnia, restless sleep, and irregular sleep-wake patterns. Poor sleep can exacerbate other mental health issues and significantly impact daily functioning. Establishing consistent bedtime routines, creating a conducive sleep environment, and addressing any underlying medical issues can help improve sleep quality.

Gastrointestinal (GI) Issues

Although not a mental health condition per se, gastrointestinal problems are frequently reported in individuals with autism and can have a significant impact on overall well-being. Chronic GI issues can contribute to irritability, anxiety, and behavioral problems. Addressing these physical health concerns through dietary modifications and medical treatment can lead to improvements in both physical and mental health.

Mental Health Interventions and Therapies
Effectively addressing mental health in individuals with autism requires a multifaceted approach that takes into account the unique needs of each person. Here are some evidence-based interventions and therapies that can help manage co-occurring mental health conditions:

Cognitive Behavioral Therapy (CBT)

Cognitive behavioral therapy (CBT) is a popular treatment modality that assists people in recognizing and altering harmful thought patterns and behaviors. Modified CBT techniques have been developed to accommodate the specific needs of individuals with ASD, focusing on visual aids, structured sessions, and concrete examples. CBT can be particularly effective in managing anxiety and depression by teaching coping strategies and problem-solving skills.

Applied Behavior Analysis (ABA)

ABA is a well-established intervention for autism that uses principles of behavior modification to teach new skills and reduce challenging behaviors. ABA techniques can also be applied to address co-occurring mental health conditions, such as anxiety and OCD, by reinforcing positive behaviors and reducing maladaptive responses.

Medication

In some cases, medication may be necessary to manage severe symptoms of co-occurring mental health conditions. Selective serotonin reuptake inhibitors (SSRIs) are commonly prescribed for anxiety and depression, while stimulants and non-stimulants may be used for ADHD. It is important to work closely with a healthcare provider to monitor the effectiveness and potential side effects of any medication.

Mindfulness and Relaxation Techniques

Mindfulness practices, such as meditation, deep breathing exercises, and progressive muscle relaxation, can help individuals with autism manage stress and anxiety. These techniques promote relaxation and self-awareness, providing tools to cope with overwhelming situations. Incorporating mindfulness into daily routines can lead to long-term improvements in mental health.

Social Skills Training

Social skills training programs are designed to help individuals with ASD develop the social and communication skills necessary for interacting with others. These programs often include role-playing, modeling, and direct instruction to teach specific social behaviors. Improved social skills can reduce anxiety in social situations and enhance overall well-being.

Family Support and Education

Family involvement is crucial in the treatment and support of individuals with autism. Educating family members about ASD and co-occurring mental health conditions can improve understanding and foster a supportive environment. Family therapy can also address any relational issues and provide strategies for managing stress and enhancing family dynamics.

Occupational Therapy (OT)

OT focuses on helping individuals with autism develop the skills needed for daily living and independent functioning. For those with co-occurring mental health conditions, occupational therapists can provide sensory integration therapy, stress management techniques, and strategies for improving executive functioning. These interventions can enhance overall quality of life and reduce the impact of mental health issues.

Holistic Approaches and Lifestyle Modifications
In addition to traditional therapies, holistic
approaches and lifestyle modifications can play a
significant role in supporting mental health and
well-being in individuals with autism.

Nutrition and Diet

*Mental health can be significantly impacted by
eating a balanced diet. Some individuals with
autism may benefit from specific dietary
interventions, such as gluten-free or casein-free
diets, although more research is needed to
confirm their efficacy. Ensuring adequate intake
of essential nutrients, such as omega-3 fatty acids,
vitamins, and minerals, can support brain health
and improve mood and behavior.*

Chapter 17

Testimonial Success Stories: Across the Lifespan

Autism Spectrum Disorder (ASD) is often portrayed through statistics and clinical observations, but behind every number and diagnosis lies a unique story of resilience, growth, and triumph. In this chapter, we share a collection of testimonial success stories that highlight the experiences of individuals with autism across different stages of life. These stories offer insight, inspiration, and hope to families, educators, and the broader community.

The Early Years: Overcoming Challenges

Regina's Journey: From Non-Verbal to Communicator

Regina was diagnosed with autism at the age of two. Her parents noticed early on that she was not reaching the same developmental milestones as other children her age. She rarely made eye contact and had significant difficulty with verbal communication. The diagnosis came as a relief and a challenge for Regina's parents, who were eager to find ways to support her development.

Regina's family engaged with early intervention services, including speech therapy, occupational therapy, and applied behavior analysis (ABA). Her parents learned to use picture exchange communication systems (PECS) and simple sign language to facilitate communication. Over time, Regina began to use these tools to express her needs and desires.

By the age of five, Regina started using a tablet with a speech-generating app, which further enhanced her ability to communicate. Her progress was remarkable; she went from being completely non-verbal to expressing herself in full sentences. Regina's story underscores the importance of early intervention and the profound impact it can have on a child's development.

Jason's Story: Thriving in an Inclusive Classroom

Jason was diagnosed with autism just before entering kindergarten. His parents were concerned about how he would adapt to the school environment, especially given his sensory sensitivities and difficulties with social interactions. However, they were committed to providing him with an inclusive educational experience.

Jason's school embraced an inclusive model, which meant he was placed in a general education classroom with appropriate supports. He had access to a special education teacher, a sensory room, and a structured routine that helped him navigate the school day. His teachers received training on how to support students with autism, and his classmates were educated about autism in an age-appropriate manner.

Over time, Jason flourished. He made friends, participated in classroom activities, and excelled academically. His parents were thrilled to see him thrive in an environment that valued diversity and inclusion. Jason's story highlights the benefits of inclusive education and the positive outcomes that can result from a supportive school community.

Adolescence: Navigating the Teenage Years

Mirabel's Success: Building Social Skills and Confidence

Mirabel was diagnosed with autism during her early teenage years. Middle school was a challenging time for her, marked by difficulties in social interactions and a feeling of being misunderstood by her peers. However, her story took a positive turn when she joined a social skills group specifically designed for teenagers with autism.

In the group, Mirabel learned valuable skills such as initiating conversations, understanding social cues, and managing anxiety. The group provided a safe space for her to practice these skills and build friendships with peers who shared similar experiences. Outside of the group, she applied what she learned in real-world settings, gradually gaining confidence and independence.

Mirabel's newfound skills and confidence led her to participate in school clubs and extracurricular activities. She became an active member of the school's robotics team, where she found a supportive community and a passion for engineering. Mirabel's story demonstrates the transformative power of targeted social skills training and the importance of fostering a sense of belonging.

Liam's Leap: Preparing for Adulthood

Liam's transition to high school was accompanied by a focus on preparing for adulthood. Diagnosed with autism at a young age, Liam's parents and educators collaborated to create a transition plan that included vocational training, life skills development, and career exploration.

Liam enrolled in a vocational program that offered hands-on training in various trades, including woodworking, culinary arts, and computer programming. He discovered a particular interest in computer programming and was encouraged to pursue internships and part-time work in the field. Additionally, Liam participated in life skills classes where he learned essential tasks such as budgeting, cooking, and using public transportation.

The support and opportunities provided to Liam allowed him to build a strong foundation for his future. Upon graduating from high school, he secured a job as a junior software developer at a local tech company. Liam's story highlights the importance of early planning and skill development in facilitating a smooth transition to adulthood for individuals with autism.

Adulthood: Achieving Independence and Success

Michael's Milestone: Independent Living

Michael's journey with autism continued into adulthood, marked by his determination to live independently. Diagnosed in childhood, Michael received extensive support from his family and various service providers. As he approached adulthood, he expressed a strong desire to live on his own.

Michael participated in a supported living program that provided him with the necessary skills and confidence to achieve his goal. He learned to manage household chores, handle finances, and navigate community resources. The program also offered social and recreational activities, allowing Michael to build a network of friends and supporters.

With time, Michael moved into his own apartment. He found employment at a local grocery store, where he enjoyed interacting with customers and colleagues. Michael's achievement of independent living is a testament to his perseverance and the effectiveness of structured support programs.

Emma's Entrepreneurial Endeavor

Emma was diagnosed with autism in her early twenties. Despite facing numerous challenges, she possessed a creative spirit and a passion for art. Determined to turn her passion into a career, Emma decided to start her own business.

With the support of a business mentor and a local entrepreneurship program, Emma launched an online store selling her handmade jewelry and artwork. She utilized social media to market her products and connected with a community of artists and customers who appreciated her unique creations.

Emma's business flourished, and she expanded her product line to include custom pieces and art workshops. Her success not only provided her with financial independence but also allowed her to share her talent and creativity with the world. Emma's story illustrates the potential for individuals with autism to achieve entrepreneurial success and make meaningful contributions to society.

Conclusion: Embracing the Journey

The testimonial success stories shared in this chapter represent just a few of the countless journeys of individuals with autism. Each story is unique, reflecting the diverse experiences and strengths of people on the autism spectrum. These narratives highlight the importance of early intervention, inclusive education, targeted support, and community involvement in fostering positive outcomes.

By sharing these stories, we hope to inspire others to recognize the potential and capabilities of individuals with autism. With the right support and opportunities, people with autism can lead fulfilling and successful lives, contributing to their communities in meaningful ways. The journey of autism is one of resilience, growth, and triumph—a journey that deserves to be celebrated and embraced.

Made in the USA
Las Vegas, NV
21 October 2024

10187438R00089